MW01073687

A IS FOR ADOBO

ABCs of FILIPINO CULTURE

BY G.M. REYES

ILLUSTRATED BY: TWINKLE A

For

Tala, my star
Elias, my home
Vera, my truth

A is for ADOBO

EVERYONE'S FAVORITE FOOD!
TAKE A DEEP BREATH,
NOTHING SMELLS AS GOOD!

SOY SAUCE AND VINEGAR,
CHICKEN AND PORK,
EAT WITH A HOT BED OF RICE,
USE A SPOON AND A FORK!

B is for BORACAY

THE BEST BEACH IN THE COUNTRY!
YOU CAN SWIM IN THE CLEAR WATERS,
OR RELAX UNDER A PALM TREE.

GO KITE SURFING, OR BUILD
CASTLES IN THE SAND.
THEN WATCH THE BEAUTIFUL
SUNSET FIRSTHAND!

C is for the
CHOCOLATE HILLS
FOUND IN BOHOL.
COUNTLESS HILLS SPREAD ACROSS THE LAND,
OVER A THOUSAND IN ALL!

BROWN DURING THE DRY SEASON,
IN THE WET SEASON THEY TURN GREEN.
THEY LOOK JUST LIKE THOSE
CHOCOLATES YOU GET ON HALLOWEEN!

D is for DURIAN

THE SMELLIEST FRUIT THERE IS.
DON'T LET THE SMELL FOOL YOU,
THE TASTE IS NOT TO MISS!

IN THE REGION OF DAVAO
IS WHERE THIS SPINY FRUIT GROWS.
YOU SHOULD DEFINITELY TRY IT,
JUST COVER YOUR NOSE!

E is for ESKRIMA

THE NATIONAL MARTIAL ART.
FROM THE ANCIENT WARRIORS
CALLED PINTADOS, IT GOT ITS START.

ANYBODY WITH PASSION
CAN NOW GO AND TAKE PART.
YOU'LL NEED TWO KALI STICKS,
AND A FIERY FILIPINO HEART.

F is for FIESTA

FULL OF CELEBRATION, COLOR, AND FUN.
YOU HAVEN'T EXPERIENCED FILIPINO
CULTURE UNTIL YOU ATTEND ONE!

EVERY PROVINCE HAS THEIR OWN RITUAL,
AND THEIR OWN DECORATIONS TOO!
LIKE THE ATI-ATIHAN IN AKLAN,
AND THE SINULOG IN CEBU!

G is for GIGIL

AN OVERWHELMING EMOTION.
IN ENGLISH IT'S CALLED
"CUTENESS AGGRESSION".

WHEN YOU SEE A SMALL PUPPY
OR A BABY SNUGGLED TIGHT,
YOU GET AN URGE TO PINCH,
TO SQUEEZE OR EVEN TO BITE!

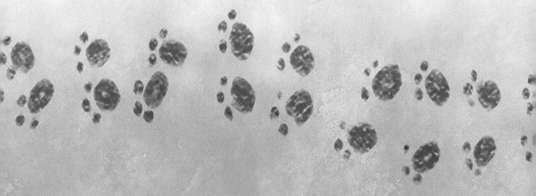

H is for HALO-HALO

WHICH LITERALLY MEANS "MIX-MIX"
ONE TASTE OF THIS DESSERT, AND
YOU'LL WANT YOUR NEXT FIX.

IT'S A MIX OF CRUSHED ICE,
AND MILK, AND JAM...
AND BEANS, AND FLAN,
AND ICE CREAM, AND YAM!

I is for IGOROT

A TRIBE FROM THE CORDILLERA MOUNTAIN RANGE.
THEY'VE LIVED FOR 500 YEARS,
BUT THEIR CULTURE IS WITHOUT CHANGE!

THEIR ANCESTORS CARVED RICE TERRACES
ALONG THE MOUNTAINSIDE.
THE BANAUE RICE TERRACES
ARE NOW A SOURCE OF NATIONAL PRIDE!

J is for JEEPNEY

OUR FAVORITE TRANSPORTATION.
WE RIDE THEM TO TRAVEL
ACROSS THE NATION.

ADORNED WITH PAINT AND
DECORATIONS THAT CATCH THE EYE,
IT'S A RAINBOW OF COLORS
AS THEY PASS BY!

K is for KALABAW

A FARMER'S BEST FRIEND.
THEY HELP PLOW THE FIELDS
AND WORK 'TIL DAY'S END.

KALABAWS ENJOY BATHING
IN MUD OR GRAZING.
THEY EVEN COMPETE IN
KALABAW RACING!

L is for LUMPIA

THE FILIPINO PARTY FAVORITE!
YOU CAN'T EAT JUST ONE,
YOU SIMPLY CAN'T CONTROL IT.

TIGHTLY WRAPPED ROLLS
WITH PORK AND VEGGIES INSIDE,
THEY TURN CRISPY GOLDEN BROWN
ONCE THEY'RE DEEP FRIED!

M is for MANGO

THE SWEETEST ONES YOU'LL EVER TASTE.
IF YOU HAVEN'T TRIED ONE,
YOU SHOULD MAKE HASTE!

ALONG EVERY STREET YOU'LL
SEE THEIR TREES TAKE ROOT.
THIS BRIGHT YELLOW TREAT IS OUR
COUNTRY'S NATIONAL FRUIT!

N is for NARRA

THE PHILIPPINES' NATIONAL TREE.
STRONG AND RESILIENT,
IT STANDS TALL AND FREE.

FROM ITS WOOD
WE MAKE THE STURDIEST OF THINGS.
FROM TABLES AND CHAIRS,
TO HOUSES FIT FOR KINGS!

THE FILIPINO ALPHABET HAS
TWO ADDED LETTERS, Ñ AND NG.
Ñ IS PRONOUNCED "N-YEAH!"
WHILE NG IS JUST LIKE THE TWO LETTERS YOU SEE!

Ñ SOUNDS LIKE THE "NI" IN "JUNIOR",
WHILE NG SOUNDS JUST LIKE THE "NG" IN "RING" TOO.
TWO BRAND NEW LETTERS,
NOW YOU LEARNED SOMETHING NEW!

O is for OPO

WHICH SIMPLY MEANS "YES" YOU USE IT WHEN IT'S ELDERS YOU ADDRESS.

OPO

IT'S A SIMPLE WORD
BUT HAS GREAT EFFECT
IT'S DISTINCTLY FILIPINO,
AND IS A SIGN OF RESPECT.

P is for PANDESAL

OUR FAVORITE BREAD.
BEST EATEN IN THE MORNING,
BEFORE THE DAY AHEAD.

FILLED WITH CHEESE OR BUTTER
OR NOTHING AT ALL,
YOU GET SO MUCH DELIGHT
FROM SOMETHING SO SMALL!

Q is for QUESO DE BOLA

A TRADITION FOR THE HOLIDAYS.
IT'S A BIG BALL OF CHEESE,
EATEN IN SO MANY WAYS.

IT'S BIG AND IT'S HEAVY,
WE BUY IT BY THE KILOGRAM,
IN NOCHE BUENA WE LIKE
TO EAT IT WITH HAM!

S is for SAMPAGUITA

THE NATIONAL FLOWER.
GARLANDS ARE SOLD IN THE STREETS,
NO MATTER THE HOUR.

ITS SWEET-SMELLING SCENT
IS A THING OF BEAUTY.
IT'S A SYMBOL OF HOPE,
STRENGTH AND PURITY.

T is for TABO

OUR FAVORITE BATHROOM TOOL!
EVERY FILIPINO HAS ONE.
THAT IS A RULE.

WITH SOAP, A BUCKET, AND WATER
THEY FORM A GOOD GROUP.
YOU CAN USE IT FOR BATHING
OR WASHING AWAY POOP!

U is for UBE

A VIBRANTLY COLORED PURPLE YAM.
WE USE IT TO MAKE CAKES,
PASTRIES, BREAD, AND JAM.

ITS COLOR AND TEXTURE SIMPLY
CAN'T BE BEAT.
IT'S OUR FAVORITE INGREDIENT
FOR EVERY SWEET TREAT!

V is for VISAYAS

ALONG WITH MINDANAO AND LUZON,
FORM THE THREE MAJOR ISLAND
GROUPS OF THE NATION.

THEY CONTAIN ALL SEVEN THOUSAND
ISLANDS IN THIS COUNTRY OF OURS.
THEY'RE SYMBOLIZED IN OUR FLAG
BY THREE YELLOW STARS.

W is for
WHALE SHARK

OR BUTANDING,
THE WORLD'S LARGEST FISH.
YOU CAN GO TO OSLOB AND
SWIM WITH THEM IF YOU WISH!

THEY GROW AS BIG AS A BUS,
EATING ONLY SHRIMP AND KRILL.
SEEING ONE UP CLOSE
IS REALLY A THRILL!

X is for XYLOPHONE

THE FILIPINO VERSION IS THE KULINTANG. BRONZE GONGS ARE HIT WITH A STICK AS THEY CLING AND CLANG

THE KULINTANG IS PLAYED
FROM ANCIENT TIMES UNTIL NOW,
IN RITUALS AND CEREMONIES BY THE
MUSLIM TRIBES IN MINDANAO.

Y is for YOYO

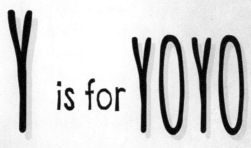

IN THE 1920'S IT CAME INTO FAME.
A FILIPINO POPULARIZED IT
AND GAVE IT ITS NAME.

PEDRO FLORES HAD PATENTS
ON THE YOYO HE DESIGNED,
WHICH PIONEERED TRICKS LIKE SLEEP,
ROCK THE BABY AND REWIND.

Z is for ZAMBALES

A PLACE TO SURF AND DIVE.
IT'S A SHORT TRIP FROM MANILA,
JUST A THREE HOUR DRIVE.

YOU CAN RIDE THE WAVES,
JUST MAKE SURE YOU DON'T SLIP!
GO SCUBA DIVING, AND SEE A
WORLD WAR II WARSHIP!

And those are some things
that Filipinos are known for.
aren't you glad
that today you learned more?

Thanks for coming with us,
so long and goodbye!
As they say in Tagalog
Paalam and Mabuhay!

Printed in the USA
CPSIA information can be obtained
at www.ICGtesting.com
LVHW071909031123
762894LV00019B/998